F R A N K
L L O Y D
W R I G H T
M I D W E S T
P O R T F O L I O

Text & Photographs by
Thomas A. Heinz

GIBBS·SMITH
P
PUBLISHER

SALT LAKE CITY

This book is dedicated to Walter L. Creese, my former professor at the University of Illinois, Urbana. It was due to his encouragement that I took up my study of Frank Lloyd Wright, and it was his insights that made me take second, third, and fourth looks at things and ideas. I am grateful for his friendship.

96 95 94 93 8 7 6 5 4 3 2 1

This is a Peregrine Smith Book, published by
Gibbs Smith, Publisher
P.O. Box 667
Layton, Utah 84041

Cover photograph: Herbert F. Johnson House, © 1993 by Thomas A. Heinz
Design by J. Scott Knudsen, Park City, Utah
Printed by Regent Publishing Services, Hong Kong

Library of Congress Cataloging-in-Publication Data
Heinz, Thomas A.
  Frank Lloyd Wright portfolio. Midwest/Thomas A. Heinz.
    p.   cm.
  ISBN 0-87905-577-4 (pbk.)
  1. Architecture, Domestic—Middle West. 2. Prairie school
(Architecture) 3. Wright, Frank Lloyd, 1867–1959—Themes, motives.
I. Title.
NA7218.H45 1993
728'.37'092—dc20   93–2195
                                                              CIP

INTRODUCTION

FRANK LLOYD WRIGHT'S life began in the Midwest, and he was buried here. Likewise, his building career began here with the construction of Hillside School for his aunts and concluded with some final remodeling of Taliesin. The vast majority of Wright buildings are located here, especially early buildings of the Prairie era.

When Wright's work is viewed as art, many often think of him as a lone practitioner. Actually, the client is the one responsible for the work getting built, since the client pays for both the design and the construction. While Wright created about a thousand designs, projects were built for only about three hundred clients. That number of clients seems very small when one thinks of how popular and well-published Wright was at certain periods in his long career.

The majority of the designs were for residences because that is what people asked him to design. It is obvious, given the body of knowledge that exists, that Wright would design anything that was requested of him. There are examples of whole communities, bridges, parking garages, furniture, dinnerware, women's dresses, books, magazine covers, and even dog houses. Each solution shows a creative approach coupled with Wright's eagerness to explore new areas without limiting himself in any direction.

Nearly fifty Wright structures are publicly accessible. There are buildings designed by Frank Lloyd Wright in thirty-six states, Canada, and Japan. Most of the Midwest houses are still used as residences.

Thomas A. Heinz
Wingspread, Racine, Wisconsin
June 1992

WARREN HICKOX HOUSE, EAST FRONT

When this house was built, Kankakee was a popular day-trip and an easy train ride from Chicago. Next door to the Hickox House, on the Kankakee River, is another Wright design built at the same time for other family members. Both the Hickoxes and the Bradleys were related to Oak Park resident and Wright client Charles Roberts. The second-floor windows are actually only two full-length windows and one pair of half size. The taper of the roof and the canted fascia board make the roof appear thin and gives the house an oriental feeling.

WARD W. WILLITS HOUSE, WEST FRONT ELEVATION

Very little appears to have changed on this house over the last ninety years, although the current owner has invested maximum effort and expense to keep the house looking the same as it did originally. The Willits House was the first of Wright's grand Prairie houses. Mr. Willits was an executive of a brass and bronze foundry that also employed Orlando Giannini, the glassmaker. Willits was a founding member of Ravinia, an early outdoor music pavilion, not far from the house, that is still a popular summer entertainment location.

SUSAN LAWRENCE DANA HOUSE, SOUTH FRONT ELEVATION

The largest residential commission at the time of its construction, this house was actually a "remodeling" and incorporates a smaller Italianate-style brick house within its new walls. The house has had a hard life and was virtually abandoned for fifteen years before a sympathetic medical-book publisher purchased it and brought it back. It has now been purchased at an extremely low price by the State of Illinois and has undergone an extensive amount of work.

Susan Lawrence Dana House, Reception Hall

This level connects all of the public rooms. The bedrooms and servants' quarters are on the second level. The terra-cotta fountain has a light behind the water spout that makes the splashing water appear to have light dancing in it as it flows into the pool. To the right is a two-story dining room and behind and to the left is the entry. The brass rods at each opening—windows, doors, between brick piers—had velvet draperies that softened the use of brick on the interior and could close off unused rooms, reducing the amount of heat required for the house.

SUSAN LAWRENCE DANA HOUSE, DINING ROOM

This composition was first seen in the 1911 Wasmuth portfolio. All the essential elements of the house are present. The tall-back dining chair is one of Wright's finest designs, but the armed variation does not seem as pleasant a mixture of elements. The sumac mural was painted by George M. Niedeken of Milwaukee, who later became a major source for Wright-designed furnishings, including rugs and table linens. What has become known as the butterfly chandelier is a complex three-dimensional piece that has no parallel in the rest of Wright's work.

SUSAN LAWRENCE DANA HOUSE, BALLROOM INGLENOOK

A pavilion at the west side of the house contains the ballroom on the second level and a library below it. At the west end of each room is a fireplace. Above this fireplace is a balcony that overlooks the ballroom. The two benches are not built-ins. They take the angle of the fireplace facing on each end. These angles are further reflected in the border and the geometry of the art-glass ceiling light above. The fireplace screen is one of several unique Wright designs in the house. Wall sconces light the short hallways leading to a small food preparation area behind the fireplace.

Susan Lawrence Dana House, Flower-in-the-Crannied-Wall Sculpture

This terra-cotta figure and finial were modeled by sculptor Richard Bock after a design by Wright. It is opposite the front entry door and greets all visitors who enter. At one time there was a small block in the fingers of the statue's right hand, making it a bit more obvious that she is building the finial. The terra-cotta was fired by William Gates at the Teco Pottery at Terra Cotta, Illinois, part of the American Terra Cotta Company. Wright designed very few sculptures. These include the capitals at the entrance to his Oak Park Studio, the bronze figures in the teller area of the bank in Mason City, and the sprites for Midway Gardens in Chicago.

FRANK L. SMITH BANK, EAST FRONT ELEVATION

Dwight, Illinois, is just west of Kankakee on another railroad line from Chicago. Colonel Smith housed both a bank and his real estate offices in here, although the building was remodeled some years ago to be exclusively a bank. The scale of this building is deceiving. The lights at either side of the front door are more than five feet above ground. It looks like a person should be able reach up and touch the upper lintel, but it is nearly twelve feet up.

THOMAS P. HARDY HOUSE, WEST STREET ELEVATION

As with nearly all of Wright's designs that are close to a busy street, this house's back is turned to the street. This affords considerable privacy for the residents and allows a great openness for the opposite side. The Hardy's easterly view was a spectacular one from the two-story space and two-story windows that overlook Lake Michigan from the top of the high bluff. Mr. Hardy was the mayor of Racine early in this century. The Hardy House is just a few blocks east of the Johnson Wax Administration Building.

Unity Temple, Lake Street Elevation

When Wright conceived of a building, that idea included all of the details and structural requirements. The roof of Unity Temple is a clever grid of concrete beams and slabs. The columns that hold up the roof are hollow and allow the ventilation for the major rooms to flow through them. The high windows allow light to pour into the auditorium and the high wall keeps out the street noises. The scale of the building is deceiving. A normal-sized person is about the same height as the building's base.

E. A. GILMORE HOUSE, NORTH ELEVATIONS

S ited atop the tallest hill in Madison, this house gives all occupants dramatic views of the capital city of Wisconsin and the numerous lakes in and around the city. Often referred to as the "Airplane House," it gives one the impression that the structure is just up to speed and ready to launch into the wild blue yonder. The house has been blessed with few owners. It remains in nearly original condition.

FREDERICK C. ROBIE HOUSE, WOODLAWN ELEVATION

This is the most famous of Wright's Prairie designs. The house is an engineering feat: the steel I-beams and channels used in the roof allowed Wright to extend the cantilevers to be thinner and longer than if he had used standard wood joists. The living room/dining room level is raised and provides an unexpectedly good view of the surroundings. Unfortunately, the house is now part of a neighborhood that has become built up, and long views are limited. Full-grown trees now obscure the house almost entirely. The house is owned by the University of Chicago.

E. P. Irving House, South Elevation

Few street elevations in Wright's long career are as symmetrical as that of the Irving House. There is a delightful concrete patio just outside the French doors on the first floor. Wright was not shy about the size of the decorative elements; the flower urns on the patio are nearly six feet wide. There is a decorative frieze, similar to the one at the Coonley House, on the second floor in the rear. Many of the final design details of this house were completed by Marion Mahoney after Wright left for Europe with Mrs. Cheney to complete the famous Wasmuth portfolio.

CITY NATIONAL BANK AND HOTEL, NORTH ELEVATION

R iver City contains several of the best Prairie houses designed by Walter Burley Griffin, William Drummond, and Frank Lloyd Wright. The city's fame came from its being the city in the story of *The Music Man*. This building is on the south side of the central city square. The bank has undergone extensive remodeling, but the hotel looks much as it did right after its completion.

A. D. German Warehouse, Frieze Detail

This former warehouse is in downtown Richland Center, Wisconsin, Frank Lloyd Wright's birthplace. The design concept sits squarely between the concepts of Midway Gardens and the Mayan influences exemplified in his concrete-block houses of Los Angeles. The thin, vertical slits are windows for the top floor.

F. C. Bogk House, West Front Elevation

T he plan of the house comes directly from Wright's earlier "Fireproof House for $5,000," published nine years earlier in the *Ladies Home Journal*. The entire front is the living room, half of the back of the first floor is the dining room, and the other half is the kitchen. There is a little sun room with balcony above in the center of the south (right) wall. This seems to be a design study for the much-larger Imperial Hotel, since the two buildings have so many design parallels.

F. C. BOGK HOUSE, WEST FRONT FRIEZE

Midway Gardens, the Chicago beer garden, had many concrete sprites in and around the building that were abstractions of the human figure. As with the Midway statues, the figure here is holding a set of cubes in its hands. Perhaps the blocks are expressions of building construction. The faces are at the very top and have expressions much like those on the sprites at the Imperial Hotel. Unlike those at Midway, these figures appear to have wings at the shoulders.

ARTHUR MUNKWITZ DUPLEX APARTMENTS, WEST FRONT ELEVATION

The City of Milwaukee decided to demolish these fine examples of low-cost housing when it widened the street. These buildings were an outgrowth of Wright's work on precut construction systems. The apartments were modest in size but uncommon in design. Delightful details and surprising uses and locations of fenestration made these apartments enjoyable places to live.

HILLSIDE HOME SCHOOL, SOUTH ELEVATION

The second building for Wright's aunts was built in 1902 across the road from a small gaggle of buildings known as Hillside, Wisconsin. The other structures have been gone for quite some time, but this school continues to be used. It was remodeled and expanded by Wright in the 1930s for his school of the arts. This pavilion, located at the west end of the building, contains the auditorium theater for the school. It houses performances put on by the Frank Lloyd Wright Foundation members and is a lecture hall for the summer tours.

TALIESIN, LAKE ELEVATION

With many of Wright's buildings, their relationships with their settings can change dramatically, depending on one's point of view. Here the house seems to perch at the top of the hill; yet when viewed from across the valley, it seems to be only halfway up the slope. This is a prime example of a place that cannot be described in pictures. It must be experienced. Luckily, these buildings are open for public tours.

TALIESIN, LIVING ROOM

This part of the Taliesin complex has undergone tremendous changes in the nearly sixty years that Wright lived and worked here. The space is complex without being complicated. There are many sub-spaces within a single room; in this view alone, one can count at least five. The colorful rug on the left was originally designed for a client from Long Island but installed here.

TALIESIN, DRAFTING ROOM

I n this room, Wright designed the Imperial Hotel, Fallingwater, Johnson Wax, the Guggenheim Museum, and hundreds of other architectural and cultural landmarks. That in itself makes this much more important than all of the rooms that Washington slept in. Wright's rebuilding after each of two major fires improved the space, its size, and complexity.

S. C. JOHNSON WAX ADMINISTRATION BUILDING, WEST ELEVATION

F ocusing the building in on itself was intended to help focus the employees on their work. The "windows" are Pyrex glass tubes. These tubes allowed those on the inside to have a limited view of the outside and what the weather was like without allowing the full view of the passing clouds that would distract the workers. The windows also provided an insulating air space long before this idea was widely accepted.

S. C. Johnson Wax Administration Building, Aerial View

I n 1936 this building was under construction and has had many additions throughout the years. The most significant of these was the Research Tower added in the mid-1940s.

HERBERT JOHNSON HOUSE, WINGSPREAD, ROOF CANOPY

This is a real structural feat. The three continuous levels of windows allow very little room for conventional supports. The glass observatory was a suggestion of the client, either to allow his children to watch him land and take off in his plane on the adjacent airstrips or to see Lake Michigan and observe the weather.

HERBERT JOHNSON HOUSE, WINGSPREAD, LIVING ROOM

I n a single space there are five rooms. These are on three levels, and yet the space does not seem complicated. The central chimney contains five fireplaces and a portion of the ventilation system. The cabinet on the right holds an early automatic record changer. The spiral staircase continues into the lookout as shown on page 53.

HERBERT JACOBS HOUSE II, EAST PIER

This is some of the best of the stone masonry on a Wright building. Herbert and Catherine Jacobs were the primary workers and were instructed and assisted by a few local stone masons. Many of Wright's houses were constructed with the owners acting either as general contractors and/or labor. The design for this house was actually the third; the second was never built. Many of Wright's clients came back for designs of other buildings or for modifications to their existing houses.

UNITARIAN MEETING HOUSE, EAST ELEVATION

right's design concept for the form of the main auditorium was that of hands folded in prayer. The building is built without a standard concrete foundation. The stone walls are set on a nine-inch-deep gravel-filled trench that is pitched to drain any water that is present. Wright gave the first sermon when the building was dedicated.

MELVIN MAXWELL SMITH HOUSE, EAST LIVING ROOM ELEVATION

Many of Wright's Usonian houses are based on this same wall and window motif. Wright was able to convince the clients to put the minimum floor space into the bedrooms and maximize the living rooms. These tall windows and doors overlook a small lake on one of the finest building sites of all the later houses.

Annunciation Greek Orthodox Church, South Elevation

Wright won an award for the design and use of concrete in this church. The dome rests on small globes of steel, so that it can flex with its changes of shape caused by the rays of the sun. The small hemispherical windows just below the dome soften the break between the dome and the wall, as does the trellis that extends out from the wall just below them. Recently, the arched windows have been filled in with stained glass, altering the building's original quiet appearance.

❦ These properties are open for public tours.